Bible Basics

A Layman's Guide to Understanding the
Old and New Testaments

JOHN HARLOW

Scripture quotations are from the Holy Bible, New International
Version® (NIV®) unless otherwise specified. Copyright © 1973,
1978, 1984, 2011 by Biblica, Inc.® Used by permission of
Zondervan. All rights reserved worldwide. www.zondervan.com.
The "NIV" and "New International Version" are trademarks
registered in the United States Patent and Trademark Office by
Biblica, Inc.®

Additional Scripture quotations are taken from the Holy Bible,
New Living Translation, copyright © 1996, 2004, 2015 by Tyndale
House Foundation. Used by permission of Tyndale House
Publishers, Inc., Carol Stream, Illinois 60188. All rights reserved.

Additional Scripture quotations are taken from the Holy Bible,
King James Version (KJV).

ISBN: 978-179-885-332-0

1. Biblical Reference 2. Biblical Studies
3. Christian Education

CONTENTS

Preface   i

1   The Old Testament Versus the New Testament   1

2   The Bible is God's Word to Us   4

3   Which Bible do You Read?   6

4   People and Events of the Bible   9

5   The Jews are God's Chosen People   12

6   The Historical Books of the Old Testament   15

7   The Poetical Books of the Old Testament   20

8   The Prophetic Books of the Old Testament   22

9   The New Testament Books   25

10   The Ten Commandments   31

11   Sin   34

12   Forgiving, Loving God   37

13   Sacrifices – Offerings – Atonement   39

14   Jesus Christ   43

15   The Second Coming of Christ   49

16   God is Not a Pushover   52

JOHN HARLOW

17   The Concept of the Trinity   55

18   Born Again?   57

19   Is There Really a Devil?   59

20   Watch Out for Bad Doctrine!   62

21   Miracles   64

22   Great Stories in the Bible   66

23   The Book of Revelation   68

24   What's a New Christian to Do?   70

PREFACE

I started drafting Bible Basics in 1987. It was the culmination of an attempt to provide a crash course in Bible study for our children. They were soon to be emptying from the nest. Our kids were in high school and it was becoming very clear that we had not provided them with the basic Sunday school experience that we had had growing up. So you might say that this book was inspired by guilt.

I started "Dad's Sunday School" in 1986. Each Sunday after church I set out to teach our kids about the Bible. This required me to do a cram course each week in preparation so that the teacher could stay ahead of the class. It was an interesting time!

As a background, my wife and I had excellent exposure to Bible study under Pastor Dick Leon and his wife Carolyn at First Presbyterian Church in Spokane in the early 80s. In 1986, however, we were in Lake Oswego and a long way from the Leons. The church we were attending at the time in Lake Oswego did not have a Bible study program that was satisfactory for our needs.

We moved to Lake Oswego in 1984 to take a job in Portland that really didn't work out well for me. It was a very stressful job with a very bureaucratic bank. Frustrated and searching for solutions to the meaning of life, I got hooked on listening to two radio programs during my commute to and from work. The morning program was Through the Bible Radio by J. Vernon McGee. The evening program was The Bible Answer Man with Dr. Walter Martin. Both these fine gentlemen are now deceased. The former continues on via taped messages and a well-funded ministry. The latter continues but has been taken over by Mr. Martin's successor. Both these programs brought together the meaning of the Bible to me as well as illustrated the "counterfeit" nature of certain religions and beliefs. I frequently found myself in disbelief of what I was hearing on these radio programs. That led me to do research on the issues of concern. Doing this research exposed me to many excellent resources for Biblical study.

I was unable to finish Dad's Sunday School because of the late start ... the kids did empty the nest. I did however draft this book in order to finish the Dad's Sunday School program and give it to our kids.

I tested my written work with several individuals (ministers) who had authority in Bible study. It has tested out well. In my enthusiasm, I decided to self-publish.

The experience has been enormously valuable to me and I enjoy sharing it with other parties who are searching for answers.

John M. Harlow
2019

1

THE OLD TESTAMENT VERSUS
THE NEW TESTAMENT

The Bible is a great big book. Reading it cover to cover can be difficult. Even so, you may have a strong desire to read and understand the entire Bible. My book is going to help you. Hopefully it will clear up any confusion you may have and explain how the New and Old Testaments fit together.

The New Testament is certainly easier to understand than the Old Testament. With a better understanding the Old Testament it brings an entirely new meaning to the New Testament. It may just create a better understanding of life, too.

The New Testament is about Jesus. He was quite something. Not one historical expert has disputed his existence. Not even some of the most far out religious groups or even those scientists who don't believe in God. Without a doubt he lived. Even so, it is extremely important to understand exactly how Jesus fits in to the Old Testament. His birth is foretold hundreds of years prior to his actual birth. Was he really God? Some believe that he was just a great prophet. Father, Son and Holy Ghost...what is the meaning of the Trinity?

With the help of some very persistent Christians, I now have developed a good understanding of the Bible. Their help has been direct (education) and indirect (example). What I discovered is that the Old Testament is truly historical. I understand exactly who Jesus is. You will read about that in this book.

In the New Testament Jesus verified the importance of the Old Testament. He also substantiated the Bible as God's word to us...unchanged from the very beginning of time.

The entire Bible teaches that God is unchanging and consistent. I think that knowing this unchanging nature of God is one of the most outstanding and comforting things about the Bible. Knowing this is important because there are many non-Christians that selectively use parts of the Bible to confuse people. Whether they are using material out of context or contesting the miracles described, you will be in a position to make your own interpretation.

Jesus verified the importance of the Old Testament: "Do not think that I have come to abolish the Law or the Prophets (i.e., the Old Testament); I have not come to abolish them but to fulfill them. I tell you the truth, until heaven and earth disappear, not the smallest letter, not the least stroke of a pen, will by any means disappear from the Law until everything is accomplished." Matthew 5:17-18

He also explained the many references to him in the Old Testament: "This is what I told you while I was still with you; Everything must be fulfilled that is written about me in the Law of Moses, the Prophets and the Psalms." Luke 24:44

Jesus emphasized his consistency with God the Father: "One of the teachers of the law came and heard them debating. Noticing that Jesus had given them a good answer, he asked him, "Of all the commandments, which is the most important?" "The most important one," answered Jesus, "is this: 'Hear, O Israel, the Lord our God, is one. Love the Lord your God with all your heart and with all your soul and with all your mind and with all your strength.' The second is this: 'Love your neighbor as yourself.' There is no commandment greater than these." Mark 12:28-31

Finally, Jesus foretells of a final judgment in which he will have an instrumental role: "At that time men will see the Son of Man (i.e. Jesus) coming in clouds with great power and glory. And he will send his angels and gather his elect from the four winds, from the ends of the earth to the ends of the heavens." Mark 13:26-27

Everyone is, or should be, curious about the future coming again of Jesus.

2

The Bible is God's Word to Us

The Bible contains precisely what God wants men and women to know. That's why it is so important for all of us to be familiar with the Bible.

Actually the Bible is not one book. It is many books written by many authors over a very long period of time. The authors spanned a period of time estimated to be about 1,500 years. Imagine a collection of authors living at different times and coming up with unity of thought!

The authors of the various books of the Bible claim that God superintended, directed, and in some cases, dictated the writing. Time and critics have tested both the Old and New Testaments. They have been tested by Jews, Christians and non-believers.

In the Old Testament, God spoke directly and indirectly to some of the people (which I will touch on in more detail in later chapters). The following are some examples of God communicating to us through Old Testament writers:

"My son, if you accept my words and store up my commands within you, turning your ear to wisdom and applying your heart to understanding, and if you call out for insight and cry aloud for understanding, and if you look for it as for silver and search for it as for hidden treasure, then you will understand the fear of the Lord and find the knowledge of God. For the Lord gives wisdom, and from his mouth comes knowledge and understanding. He holds victory in store for the upright, he is a shield to those whose walk is blameless, for he guards the course of the just and protects the way of his faithful ones." Proverbs 2:1-8

"As for God, his way is perfect; the word of the Lord is flawless. He is a shield for all who take refuge in him." 2 Samuel 22:31

The consistency of God's word runs throughout the Bible. Because of the enormity of the Bible, it takes a while to discover that God hasn't changed … and doesn't go back on His word. When you are "getting your life and act together," this knowledge of an unchanging God giving us clear directions through the Bible is very valuable, important and comforting.

"All your words are true; all your righteous laws are eternal." Psalm 119:160

I deal more with how God "authored" the Bible in Chapter 21 (Miracles). Assuming that you agree that God did author the Bible, then it follows that the Bible is authoritative for us.

Again, the more you get into it, the more you realize that the Bible contains precisely what God wants men and women to know.

3

WHICH BIBLE DO YOU READ?

As I mentioned in Chapter 1, finding a Bible that is understandable can be difficult. Fortunately today there are many options available that are easier to understand than the King James Version. In fact and compared to 1950, there may be too many Bible options available. So many, that instead of having difficulty understanding the one Bible that you have, you may be having difficulty understanding why there are so many different versions and which version to pick. I can give you some insight.

As a background, the original Old Testament was written in ancient Hebrew. On the other hand, the New Testament was written in Greek which was the accepted language during the first century after Christ. To complicate matters, the early church was persecuted ruthlessly during the first few centuries after Christ. Those that did the persecution wanted to eliminate all records of the early Christian church. They also tried to eliminate those church members who would not abandon their faith in Christ. Even though gladiator fights and feeding the Christians to the lions made for some great movies to come out of Hollywood, to live through it must have been some of the worst oppression in history.

The point of this brief history lesson has been to point out that preserving the books of the Bible from the time of Jesus down to today has not been an orderly task. Some documents substantiating the accuracy of the Bible are still popping up (Dead Sea Scrolls).

Of the plethora of Bibles available, let me illustrate to you the difference regarding the telling of the same story. I have chosen a familiar excerpt from Matthew regarding the birth of Christ (1:18-19).

New International Version: "This is how the birth of Jesus Christ came about: His mother Mary was pledged to be married to Joseph, but before they came together, she was found to be with child through the Holy Spirit. Because Joseph her husband was a righteous man and did not want to expose her to public disgrace, he had in mind to divorce her quietly."

King James Version: "Now the birth of Jesus Christ was on this wise: When as his mother Mary was espoused to Joseph, before they came together, she was found with child of the Holy Ghost. Then Joseph her husband, being a just man, and not willing to make her a public example, was minded to put her away privily."

The Living Bible: "These are the facts concerning the birth of Jesus Christ: His mother, Mary, was engaged to be married to Joseph. But while she was still a virgin she became pregnant by the Holy Spirit. Then Joseph, her fiancé, being a man of stern principle, decided to break the engagement but to do it quietly, as he didn't want to publicly disgrace her."

As you can see, these versions say the same thing; however, the ease of understanding varies greatly.

When researching Bibles, it's important to know the difference between **translations** and **paraphrases**. A translation is an English language version of the Bible taken directly from the "original" documents. The translation represents the most accurate Bible, getting God's word to us exactly as He delivered it ... word for word. An obvious problem with a translation is to determine which "original" documents were used. Also, there are disputes whether the interpreter chose the correct way of saying something in today's language when the original was written in Greek or Hebrew. The difficulty of this task is compounded because a lot of expressions and terms cannot be duplicated from one language to another.

A paraphrase is a "restatement of a text or passage in other words, often to clarify meaning"... to use my dictionary's words. Certainly the paraphrase reads better. A paraphrase is usually very close to a translation. The paraphrase restates the "original" documents more in terms of thought for thought rather than word for word. The paraphraser's goal is to make the Bible more understandable ... it is not necessarily to bring you God's word exactly as originally recorded. In my opinion, some of the more popular Bibles that claim to be a translation in their Preface or Introduction are actually a paraphrase. There is nothing wrong with a paraphrase.

In summary, for easy reading or for the novice Bible student, a paraphrase is wonderful. For deeper study of God's word or for prayerful meditation, I believe that a good word for word translation should be used.

The following are examples of translations that exist today: King James Version; New International Version; New American Standard Version; New American Translation; The Jerusalem Bible; The Revised Standard Version; and the New English Bible.

These Bibles are paraphrases: J.B. Phillips' Bible in Modern English; The Good News Bible (Today's English Bible); and The Living Bible (The Book).

In this book, I have chosen to quote from the New International Version.

You need to be aware that there are counterfeits. Although I am not an expert in determining a counterfeit, these counterfeits seem to occur with some cults and/or singular denominations. Critical portions of the Bible are changed so that their Bible agrees with idiosyncrasies of their religious beliefs. For this reason, be certain that the Bible you choose has been recommended by multidenominational Biblical scholars.

4

PEOPLE AND EVENTS OF THE BIBLE

Later chapters will give you a quick look at what is contained in each of the books of the Bible. In this chapter, I take you through a chronology of the more notable people and events covered in the Bible.

I believe it will be very helpful in your understanding to have a feeling for the large time frame covered in the Bible. As well, it is important to know who followed whom in Biblical history. The dates I have used are not intended to be exact. There seems to be considerable debate over exact dates. The further you go back in time, the more the dates are subject to challenge due to limited archeological proof. In any event what follows is a rough time-frame.

"Pre-History"
God created the first man – Adam. Adam's sons were Cain, Able, Seth, and many more.

2400BC (or First Biblically Datable Period)
This is the time of Noah and the Flood which destroyed most forms of life that did not make it on the Ark. Something must have gone drastically wrong in the years between the time of Adam and Noah for God to have made this severe a judgment on the world.

2000BC

Abraham, the first Jew, was called by God when he was living in modern day Iraq. The area is near the mouths of the Tigress and Euphrates Rivers which empty into the Persian Gulf. Over time Abraham migrated to the land of Canaan (modern day Israel) which is about a 1,000 mile journey. Abraham's son was Isaac. Isaac's son was Jacob whose name was changed by God to Israel. Israel's sons became the namesakes for the twelve tribes of Israel. Over 400 years later, Moses distributed the land in Israel to the twelve tribes.

1400BC

Moses led the Jews out of Egypt. The Jews migrated to Egypt years earlier as a result of a severe drought in Israel. They grew in numbers and eventually fell into slavery in Egypt. This slavery lasted for a couple hundred years until God rescued them from their captivity by using Moses. The Lord performed several miracles through Moses.

It is interesting that God talked directly with Moses. The best known discourse involves the presentation of the Ten Commandments. Other than Moses, most communications from God recorded in the Bible were indirect. Examples on indirect would be by dreams or from angels.

1000BC

King David reigned over Israel during the best of times for the Jews. Later, at the time of Christ, the Jews expected that the Messiah would come and establish a kingdom on earth that would surpass King David's.

During the 400 years between the times of Moses and David, the Jews re-inhabited Israel and gradually built up their country and government. In terms of wealth and prosperity, Israel's peak occurred under David's son, King Solomon.

As wealth, greed, idolatry, immorality, ungodliness, etc. crept into the nation Israel, the government, and nation, slowly began to deteriorate. The further they drifted from God, the more the nation struggled and deteriorated.

800 to 400BC

This was the time of the Prophets, all sixteen of them. The purpose of the Prophets was to warn Gods people of their fate if they continued their sinful ways. The warnings went mostly unheeded and Israel fell from the good graces of God. This fall eventually resulted in the destruction of Jerusalem by powerful enemies and another long exile. This time it was to Babylonia in the same general area of Abraham's origin. Some of the well-known Prophets were: Daniel, Jonah, Isaiah, Jeremiah and Ezekiel. We'll talk more about the prophets in Chapter 8.

400BC to Christ's Birth

The Jews eventually got back to Israel from their Babylonian captivity. They rebuilt Jerusalem which had been completely destroyed. This became a period of relative prosperity for the Jews. They were ruled by several other nations – Persians, Greeks, and Romans. In between the Greeks and Romans they actually had a short period of independence. However, the Jews yearned for the independence and power of King David's empire. They looked forward to a return to this power under the Messiah foretold by the Prophets. Indeed the Messiah was to come, but not as the expected king with all powerful armies.

Christ's Birth to 100BC

This is the time covered by the New Testament. It includes the birth of Christ and his ministry on earth. There is also a history of the young Christian church and several letters (Epistles) explaining Jesus and his teachings. The last book of the New Testament is a prophesy of things yet to come.

The Jews are God's Chosen People

It is a Biblical fact that Jews were chosen by God through Abraham to be His people. Jesus was a Jew, and so were all his Apostles. Jesus was also the Messiah foretold in the Old Testament. A great many of the Jews in Christ's time understood that he was the Messiah. However, the established rulers of the Jewish church at that time did not did not accept him as the Messiah. These rulers ultimately had the Romans crucify Christ. This has been a primary source of Christian criticism and persecution of Jews since that time.

The fact that the Hebrew "church" rejected Jesus Christ actually opened the door for non-Jews to be acceptable to the Lord. In other words and according to the New Testament, the nation Israel's mistake benefited all other peoples (Gentiles).

I wrote this chapter because prior to and during my learning about the Bible, I had nagging questions about Judaism, Israel, and how Christianity fit in with both.

Jews were and *probably still are* God's chosen people. This is substantiated by Scripture. God addressed Abraham approximately 4,000 years ago: "I will make you into a great nation and I will bless you; I will make your name great, and you will be a blessing. I will bless those who bless you, and whoever curses you I will curse; and all peoples on earth will be blessed through you." Genesis 12:2-3. By the Bible stating "all peoples," that includes non-Jews. There is not a time line specified, however. It is not until the New

Testament that it is clear that God's grace has been extended to all peoples.

Likewise God addressed Abraham's son, Isaac: "I will make your descendants as numerous as the stars in the sky and will give them all these lands, and through your offspring all nations on earth will be blessed, because Abraham obeyed me and kept my commands, my decrees and my laws." Genesis 26:4-5. Again, "all nations" is all inclusive … Gentiles and Jews. The term gentiles is defined as all non-Jews.

And God reaffirmed to Isaac's son Jacob in a dream: "I am the Lord, the God of your father Abraham and the God of Isaac. I will give you and your descendants the land on which you are lying. Your descendants will spread out to the west and to the east, to the north and to the south. All people on earth will be blessed through you and your offspring. I am with you and will watch over you wherever you go, and I will not leave you until I have done what I have promised you." Genesis 28:13-15

It appears to me that God would be most pleased to have his chosen people believing in Christ and the New Testament. In light of these passages, Christians should perhaps be evangelizing as many Jews as they can.

In the 2,000 years from Abraham to Christ, a great deal of the Bible deals with the struggle between God and his chosen people. When the Jews worshipped God and made a good effort to follow His unchanging will, things went well. When the Jews drifted away from God, things did not go so well. At those times, either the Jews repented of their sins or God judged them. Some of the judgments were very severe!

When Christ came, he offered forgiveness and eternal life to the Jews. By and large, they rejected him. Based upon their scriptures (the Old Testament), they should have been prepared to receive Christ and his message.

Christ was very critical of the Jews in that they did not recognize or accept him as the Messiah. The following passages are examples:

"Then Jesus cried out, 'When a man believes in me, he does not believe in me only, but in the One who sent me. When he looks at me, he sees the One who sent me. I have come into the world as a light, so that no one who believes in me should stay in darkness. As for the person who hears my words but does not keep them, I do not judge him. For I did not come to judge the world, but to save it. There is a judge for the one who rejects me and does not accept my words; that very word which I spoke will condemn him at the last day. For I did not speak of my own accord, but the Father who sent me commanded me what to say and how to say it. I know that His command leads to eternal life. So whatever I say is just what the Father has told me to say." John 12:45-50

"O Jerusalem, Jerusalem, you who kill the prophets and stone those sent to you, how often I have longed to gather your children together, as a hen gathers her chicks under her wings, but you were not willing." Matthew 23:37

Through Christ, we are all offered the salvation and eternal life that was originally reserved for God's chosen people. Peter, Christ's apostle, makes this clear:

"The apostles and the brothers throughout Judea heard that the Gentiles also had received the word of God. ... So if God gave them the same gift as he gave us, who believed in the Lord Jesus Christ, who was I to think that I could oppose God. When they heard this, they had no further objections and praised God, saying, 'So then, God has granted even the Gentiles repentance unto life." Acts 11:1, 17-18

Paul expounds on this further: "You are all sons of God through faith in Christ Jesus, for all of you who were baptized in to Christ have clothed yourselves with Christ. There is neither Jew nor Greek, slave nor free, male nor female, for you are all one in Christ Jesus. If you belong to Christ, then you are Abraham's seed, and heirs according to the promise." Galatians 3:26-29

6

THE HISTORICAL BOOKS OF THE OLD TESTAMENT

There are 39 books in the Old Testament. The first 17 of these books are classified as Historical. These books take God's people from their very beginnings down to roughly 44BC. (See Chapter 4 for a chronology of people and events.)

The Jews were a very intelligent nation. Information was passed down from generation to generation.

There is archeological evidence (ruin, tablets, scrolls, etc.) going way back that substantiate the Biblical record. For those inclined toward ancient history and archeology, this is a very interesting area to study – verification of the Bible through science.

It is generally accepted that the first five books of the Old Testament were written approximately at the time of Moses. Some scholars debate whether Moses actually wrote these books; but in order to keep things simple, I am writing as if Moses was the author.

The first book, Genesis, is before Moses' time so Moses must have been formalizing information passed down from his Jewish ancestors.

Four out of these first five books deal with what went on in Moses' day. Moses' writings have been very important to both Christians and Jews because he recorded his frequent conversations with God. No other Biblical figure had as much conversation with God, so if you are searching to find out what God expects of us, these books by Moses are very important.

Genesis: Genesis covers the beginning of the world through Abraham to Abraham's great grandsons. Genesis ends when a drought forced Abraham's family to leave Israel and move to Egypt (approximately 2000BC). This book is generally thought to have been written by Moses from information passed down from early generations.

Exodus: Exodus picks up with the birth of Moses (approximately 1400BC) and deals with Moses' early life, the exodus of the Jews from slavery in Egypt, and the early years in the Sinai wilderness (including the giving of the Ten Commandments).

Leviticus: This book details the laws that God set up through Moses for the Jews. Although this is a very important book, it is not a favorite of beginning Bible students. If you are a beginner, I recommend that you pass on this one for the time being.

Numbers: This book covers the 40 years in which the Jews wandered in the Sinai wilderness. This is the time from shortly after the miraculous flight from Egypt up until the time the Jews occupied, or re-entered, the land of Abraham ... Israel. The Sinai does not take 40 years to walk across. God kept them there in the desolate wilderness as punishment. While in the Sinai, they broke His commandments and returned to the immoral Egyptian ways. Even so, God saw to it that their basic needs were taken care of (food, clothing, shelter, etc.).

Deuteronomy: This book is largely a repetition of the law given in earlier books. This book was written during the last year in the life of Moses. The repetition was for the benefit of the new generation of Jews coming out of the Sinai wilderness 40 years after their exodus from Egypt.

Joshua: Joshua came out of Egypt with Moses and was his right hand man. He was an excellent military leader and was undoubtedly up in years when he led the Jews into Israel after the death of Moses. Because of the sinfulness in the Sinai, God did not allow the adults who came out of

Egypt to enter the "promised land." The Jewish population increased while in the Sinai, but the 40 years allowed time for the earlier generation of exiles to pass away. Only Joshua and one other man were allowed to enter it. This book covers the entry into the Promised Land and was probably written by scribes at the time of Joshua.

Judges: This book covers the period of time from the death of Joshua up until Samuel, the prophet. The book is named after the spiritual leaders of the various tribes of Israel ... the judges. The tribes of Israel did not have a unified government. They were united under God's law, but were not united under a king until later. The book of Judges covers a period of time of approximately 200 years and was probably written by historians within a generation after the last events covered in the book.

Ruth: This is a short story about a woman who lived some time during the book of Judges. Ruth was the great grandmother of King David. The book was written by an unknown author at the time of David.

I and II Samuel: These books were also written by an unknown author or authors probably during or shortly after the time of David. The first book starts with the ministry of Samuel ... a prophet and one of the judges. It covers the establishment of the first king of Israel – Saul. The second book goes into the reign of King David. David's reign was near the peak of the Jewish kingdom and lasted some forty years. The book closes with David still living. The author(s) of Samuel was a very good story teller.

I and II Kings: Whereas the author of Samuel was writing about an upbeat time for Israel, the author of Kings was covering the decline of the kingdom. Kings covers a period of time of approximately 400 years, and Jewish tradition has the author as Jeremiah, the prophet. The first book opens with the death of King David and covers the reign of King Solomon (the wisest man and the wealthiest kingdom). It also describes a "Civil War" after the time of Solomon wherein Israel is broken into two kingdoms – the North (retaining the name of Israel) and the South (Judah). The second book closes with both kingdoms being overrun by greater powers – Assyria and Babylonia. The books were probably written in exile in Babylonia.

I and II Chronicles: These books provide repeat coverage of the events and people covered in the earlier books of Samuel and Kings with emphasis upon the spiritual more than the historical detail. Chronicles ends with the return of the Jewish people from the Babylonian captivity and exile. From this standpoint, the author of Chronicles was writing later than the author of Kings. Jewish tradition has the author of Chronicles as Ezra, a prominent Jew at the time of the end of the Babylonian exile.

Ezra and Nehemiah: These books, as well as Chronicles, are thought to have been written by the religious leader named Ezra. Jerusalem and the Temple had been destroyed when the Babylonians overran Judah. The Jews were in captivity in Babylonia for about 50 years. When the Persians conquered the Babylonians, the Persians returned the Jews to their homeland. Between Ezra and Nehemiah, these individuals saw to it that the Temple and the protective wall around Jerusalem were rebuilt. There was considerable resistance to the rebuilding, probably a result of "political" fear that the strength of David's kingdom might somehow be restored. The books of Ezra and Nehemiah tell the story of the rebuilding. The book of Nehemiah ends about 400BC which is the latest time in history covered until the New Testament takes over (see chronology in Chapter 4).

Esther: Esther was a Jewish woman who became the Queen of Persia at the time when the Persians ruled most of the known world (remember I stated above that the Persians conquered the Babylonians). Esther was instrumental in helping the Jews, particularly Nehemiah, in the rebuilding of Jerusalem.

There is an excellent summary of the Old Testament Historical Books contained in the New Testament as given by an early Christian named Stephen. Stephen was martyred by the Jews shortly after Christ was crucified. This summary is contained in a speech given by Stephen as told in Acts 7:2-47.

7

The Poetical Books of the Old Testament

The Poetical Books follow the Historical Books. They are sometimes considered the Books of Wisdom. Most of these five books have literary merit and that's why they're called Poetical. As well, most of these books were written during the greatest times of the Jewish history ... the kingdoms of David and Solomon.

Job: This is a story about a man named Job and how Satan tested Job's faith in God. The timing of when this story takes place is unknown. It could have been written during the time of David or Solomon; it also could have been written much earlier ... or later. In essence, despite terrible misfortunes that happened to Job, he managed to remain faithful to God and ultimately was rewarded for his faithfulness.

Psalms: The Psalms are truly poetry. There are 150 Psalms, all of which appear to have been written to be set to or sung with music. About half of the Psalms are known to have been written by King David. The remaining Psalms were written at various times and by various authors. The main ideas expressed in the Psalms are praising God, trusting in Him, and rejoicing in His mercy.

Psalms are used in most church services. Their messages apply today as they did 3,000 years ago. One of the most famous in Psalm 23: "The Lord is my shepherd, I shall not want ..."

Jesus frequently quoted Psalms during his earthly ministry. We assume that they were favorites of his.

Proverbs: Very similar to how half of the Psalms have been attributed to David, most of the Proverbs are attributed to Solomon. (As we mentioned earlier, Solomon was David's son and considered the wisest man.) There are approximately 900 proverbs. These are wise sayings expressing truths about practical every day affairs of life ... most are timeless.

Ecclesiastes: Written by Solomon, Ecclesiastes is very melancholy and basically illustrates the emptiness of life without God. Solomon had everything ... wealth, wisdom and power. Apparently he tried everything, too. Ecclesiastes was written for those of us who are still trying to get everything the world has to offer. This book lets us know that our attempt is in vain. If for some reason we could get everything, without God we would be empty.

Song of Solomon or Song of Songs: This is a love poem, written by Solomon to one of his wives (he had many!).

In my opinion, the Poetical Books don't have to be read to understand the Bible; although they do offer support to what the rest of the Bible teaches. The Poetical Books can be read and enjoyed at your leisure. They are a wonderful source of wisdom; and as well, they are thought provoking by posing difficult questions. The Psalms do contain several Messianic prophesies, which are very important; and, as mentioned earlier, Jesus frequently quoted from Psalms.

8

THE PROPHETIC BOOKS OF THE OLD TESTAMENT

The last 17 books of the Old Testament are referred to as the Prophetic Books. There are prophets throughout the Old Testament books. Some famous prophets do not have Old Testament books named after them. Two examples are Elijah and Elisha (no, these are not typos!).

All of the prophets for whom Old Testament books have been named lived after the reigns of King David and King Solomon. The Bible tells of the decline of Israel's power and influence as a result of the peoples' separation from God. Idolatry, immorality, worldliness – all began creeping into the nation's lifestyle. Slowly God removed his protection of the people of Israel. This separation from God occurs over a long period of time, and there are several attempts at restitution. Unfortunately, none of the reforms seem to last much longer than a generation.

The prophets spoke for God and, generally, warned the Jews of the fate that would befall them if they did not turn from their worldly ways back to Godly and holy ways. Because the prophets' words were generally at odds with the current interests of the Jewish leaders, the prophets were not always thought of kindly. Several of the prophets suffered martyrdom as a result of their unwavering faith in their message.

God knew that He would need prophets. He gave Moses instructions on how to determine a true prophet from a false prophet:

"You may say to yourselves, 'How can we know when a message has not been spoken by the Lord?' If what a prophet proclaims in the name of the Lord does not take place or come true, that is a message the Lord had not spoken. That prophet has spoken presumptuously. Do not be afraid of him." Deuteronomy 18: 21-22

"If a prophet, or one who foretells by dreams, appears among you and announces to you a miraculous sign or wonder, and if the sign or wonder of which he has spoken takes place, and he says, 'Let us follow other gods' (gods you have not known) 'and let us worship them,' you must not listen to the words of that prophet or dreamer." Deuteronomy 13: 1-3

Christ expounded further on the need to be careful of people who claim divine prophesy:

"Watch out for false prophets. They come to you in sheep's clothing, but inwardly they are ferocious wolves. By their fruit you will recognize them. Do people pick grapes from thorn bushes, or figs from thistles? Likewise every good tree bears good fruit, but a bad tree bears bad fruit. A good tree cannot bear bad fruit, and bad tree cannot bear good fruit. Every tree that does not bear good fruit is cut down and thrown into the fire. Thus, by their fruit you will recognize them." Matthew 7: 15-20

The prophets of the Old Testament frequently did not even understand the importance of their own words. Their predictions weren't entirely clear in light of the events occurring in their day. This is explained in the New Testament:

"Above all, you must understand that no prophecy of Scripture came about by the prophet's own interpretation. For prophecy never had its origin in the will of man, but men spoke from God as they were carried along by the Holy Spirit." 2 Peter 1: 20-21

The prophets who have Biblical books named after them lived over a period time covering about 300 to 400 years. The Prophetic Books are not arranged chronologically in the

Bible; however, the following is a very crude chronological listing of the Prophets arranged by me. These times are very debatable and only used to give you a rough sense of the historical time frames involved:

Amos	790-760 BC
Jonah	770-760 BC
Hosea	770-725 BC
Isaiah	740-680 BC
Micah	740-690 BC
Nahum	640-630 BC
Zephaniah	630-620 BC
Jeremiah	630-575 BC
Habakkuk	625-620 BC
Daniel	610-530 BC
Ezekiel	590-570 BC
Lamentations (by Jeremiah)	585-575 BC
Obadiah	580-570 BC
Haggai	530-520 BC
Zechariah	520-510 BC
Malachi	455-440 BC
Joel	Timeless and undated

The prophets were grouped around very significant events that occurred during these 300 to 400 years. The history of this time period is covered in the books of Kings and Chronicles. The first grouping of prophets occurred around the fall of the Northern Kingdom (Israel) which was overrun by the Assyrians (800 to 700 BC). The second group of prophets surrounded the fall of the Southern Kingdom (Judah) which was overrun by the Babylonians (650 to 550 BC). Next, there were prophets during the return of the Jews from the Babylonian captivity. This occurred in two waves, the first one in the early 500's and the second in the mid-400's BC.

9

The New Testament Books

In the period of time between the Old Testament and the New Testament, the Middle East was under the rule of three different major powers at different times. There were 400 years that transpired from the rebuilding of Jerusalem up until the birth of Jesus.

The first to rule the Jews were the Persians. The Persians allowed the Jews to return to Israel and rebuild Jerusalem. After the Persians, came the Greeks. Alexander the Great conquered not only the Middle East but most of the known world. Among other things, the Greeks are attributed with establishing a uniform language throughout the world. The early New Testament transcripts were written in Greek which enhanced the spread of Christianity.

Following the Greeks were the Romans. Wherein the Greeks used their minds or cleverness to rule the world, the Romans used force. The Roman armies built roads throughout their empire. This enabled them to move their forces efficiently. The Romans were in power when Christ was born. These same roads that were intended to control the population were also very effective in providing a means to physically spread early Christianity.

The New Testament contains 27 books. They were all written within a period of about 100 years after Christ was crucified. The New Testament books are divided into the Gospels (4), the book of Acts (1), the Epistles (21 letters), and a prophetic book (Revelation).

The Gospels deal with the life, teaching, death and resurrection of Christ. The book of Acts deals with events in the lives of some of Christ's Apostles as well as the formation of the early Christian church. The Epistles contain correspondence between early Christians. When addressed to Jewish Christians, these letters dealt with Christ being the Messiah and other interpretations of Scripture (Old Testament). When directed toward Gentiles (non-Jews), the letters dealt with eternal life and salvation through Christ.

Before going further and in order to understand the authors of the New Testament, you need to know some things about the people in Jesus' life.

While Jesus was living, the main individuals in his ministry were the twelve men he chose to follow him. They are referred to as The Twelve, the Apostles, or the Twelve Disciples.

Jesus selected his Apostles over a period of about one and one-half years. Jesus' ministry began when he was approximately 30 years old ... shortly thereafter he began selecting his Apostles. (Not coincidentally, the age of 30 was the Jewish age of spiritual leadership.) Jesus' entire public ministry lasted just a little over three years. It began with his baptism by John the Baptist and ended with his crucifixion.

The Twelve Disciples are listed in three of the Gospels as well as in Acts (Matthew 10:2-4; Mark 3:16-19; Luke 6:12-19; and Acts 1:13). They are as follows: Peter (Simon Peter), John, Matthew, Thomas, Andrew, James (brother of Andrew), Philip, Bartholomew, James (son of Alphaeus), Simon, Thaddaeus (or the other Judas), and Judas Iscariot (who betrayed Christ).

The four Gospels essentially tell about the life of Christ; however, each Gospel author had a slightly different emphasis.

The Book of Matthew: Matthew was one of the Apostles. Prior to being chosen as an Apostle, Matthew had been a tax collector. Matthew's gospel emphasizes that Jesus was the fulfillment of the Old Testament prophesies regarding the Messiah. For this reason, his gospel is thought to have been written for the benefit of the Jews and early Jewish Christians. Matthew pointed out that following Jesus did not involve repudiating that Old Testament. Rather Jesus' teachings were not only consistent with the Old Testament but that his very being was predicted in those scriptures.

The Book of Mark: Mark was not one of the Apostles. He was John Mark who was a young man at the time of Jesus' ministry. Mark apparently knew most of the Apostles and followed the apostle Peter closely after Jesus' crucifixion. For this reason, Mark's gospel is thought to be based upon Peter's accounts of Jesus. Peter was a big man and a fisherman ... one of the more colorful and prominent of The Twelve. Mark gave special emphasis to Jesus' deeds and miracles rather than Jesus being the fulfillment of the Old Testament (as Matthew did). For this reason it is thought that Mark wrote his gospel for the non-Jewish, gentile Christians who probably did not fully understand Jewish customs and history.

The Book of Luke: Luke was a physician and highly educated. He was probably Greek and not Jewish. He definitely had not known Christ while Christ was living. He was a close companion of Paul who was Jewish and who wrote most of the Epistles (see chapter on Paul later). Luke traveled extensively and apparently interviewed many Christians who had known Christ. Luke put together his gospel after very carefully gathering facts and accounts about the life of Jesus. More than the other gospels, Luke's gospel is organized as an historical record.

Luke also wrote Acts, which is a continuation of his historical record, and covers the early Christian church. Like for his gospel writing, Luke was very thorough in his fact gathering and presentation.

The Book of John: John, like Matthew, was one of the Twelve Disciples of Christ. John and Peter appear to have been closer to Jesus than the rest of the Apostles. John may have been the closest earthly friend of Jesus. John refers to himself as "the disciple whom Jesus loved" several times. John's gospel emphasizes the deity of Jesus.

The book of Revelation was also written by John wherein Jesus (long after his crucifixion) reveals to John prophetic imagery of the future. I will deal with Revelation more in a later chapter.

There are also three short Epistles written by John (I John, II John, and III John),

Paul: Paul was selected by Christ after his crucifixion. It is possible that Jesus intended for Paul to replace the apostle that betrayed Jesus – Judas Iscariot. In any event, Paul was a very devout Jewish leader. He was raised and educated by the established Jewish power structure. He was part of the same group that called for the crucifixion of Christ. Following his fellow Jewish leaders and prior to his calling by Christ, Paul was determined to destroy the early Christian church.

These verses from Acts record Paul's conversion (Note: In the passage that follows, Paul is referred to as Saul. His name was changed by Jesus from Saul to Paul after Saul's conversion. Also, the term Way refers to the early Christians.):

> Meanwhile, Saul was still breathing out murderous threats against the Lord's disciples. He went to the high priest and asked him for letters to the synagogues in Damascus, so that if he found any there who belonged to the Way, whether men or women, he might take them as prisoners to Jerusalem. As he neared Damascus on his journey, suddenly a light from heaven flashed around him. He fell to the ground and heard a voice say to him, 'Saul, Saul, why do you persecute me?' 'Who are you, Lord?' Saul asked. 'I am Jesus, whom you are

persecuting,' he replied. 'Now get up and go into the city, and you will be told what you must do.' The men traveling with Saul stood there speechless; they heard the sound but did not see anyone. Saul got up from the ground, but when he opened his eyes he could see nothing. So they led him by the hand into Damascus. For three days he was blind, and did not eat or drink anything. In Damascus there was a disciple named Ananias. The Lord called to him in a vision, 'Ananias!' 'Yes, Lord,' he answered. The Lord told him, 'Go to the house of Judas on Straight Street and ask for a man from Tarsus named Saul, for he is praying. In a vision he has seen a man named Ananias come and place his hands on him to restore his sight.' 'Lord,' Ananias answered, 'I have heard many reports about his man and all the harm he has done to your saints in Jerusalem. And he has come here with authority from the chief priests to arrest all who call on your name.' But the Lord said to Ananias, 'Go! This man is my chosen instrument to carry my name before the Gentiles and their kings and before the people of Israel. I will show him how much he must suffer for my name.' Then Ananias went to the house and entered it. Placing his hands on Saul, he said, 'Brother Saul, the Lord-Jesus, who appeared to you on the road as you were coming here-has sent me so that you may see again and be filled with the Holy Spirit.' Immediately, something like scales fell from Saul's eyes, and he could see again. He got up and was baptized, and after taking some food, he regained his strength. Saul spent several days with the disciples in Damascus. At once he began to preach in the synagogues that Jesus is the Son of God. Acts 9:1-20

James: There is one Epistle by James. He was a Jewish Christian in Jerusalem and is thought to have been the James who was Jesus' half-brother – son of Joseph and Mary. There were two Apostles named James, but this Epistle is not by either of these men.

Jude: This Epistle writer identified himself as the brother of James. He is possibly another half-brother of Jesus. (The Jewish names Jude and Judas were the same.)

Referring to Jesus in Matthew; "Isn't this the carpenter's son? Isn't his mother's name Mary, and aren't his brothers James, Joseph, Simon and Judas?" Matthew 13:55

Peter: There are two Epistles by Peter. They are thought to have been by the Apostle Peter.

Because the Epistles are letters to early churches and church members, it is helpful to read a little background on each Epistle prior to its reading. Several Bibles have introductory or indexed sections that can give you this helpful background. There are also an abundance of study aids, handbooks, etc. that provide this information.

Revelation: The book of Revelation is covered in Chapter 23.

10

The Ten Commandments

God gave the Ten Commandments to Moses almost 3400 years ago. Over Moses' lifetime, God also communicated several other directives to Moses in the form of laws, rules or standards. The Ten Commandments and all these other directives were referred to as the Law.

Keeping the Law was, and is, impossible for mortal men and women. Breaking God's Law constitutes sinning (Chapter 11). God spelled out the consequences for sinning. God provided a means of atonement for some sins as they were committed (Chapter 13 explores this further). The bottom line is that God gave the Jews firm guidelines to follow for moral, holy behavior, and He also spelled out the consequences for breaking these guidelines.

The Ten Commandments are the backbone of the Law, and they are presented in Exodus and Deuteronomy:

"And God Spoke these words: "I am the Lord your God, who brought you out of Egypt, out of the land of slavery.

1. You shall have no other gods before me.

2. You shall not make for yourselves an idol in the form of anything in heaven above or on the earth beneath or in the waters below. You shall not bow down to them or worship them; for I, the Lord your God, am a jealous God, punishing the children for the sin of the fathers to the third and fourth generation of those who hate me, but showing love to a thousand generations of those who love me and keep my commandments.

3. You shall not misuse the name of the Lord your God, for the Lord will not hold anyone guiltless who misuses His name.

4. Remember the Sabbath day by keeping it holy. Six days you shall labor and do all your work, but the seventh day is a Sabbath to the Lord your God. On it you shall not do any work, neither you, nor your son or daughter, nor your manservant or maidservant, nor your animals, nor the alien within your gates. For in six days the Lord made the heavens and the earth, the sea, and all that is in them, but He rested on the seventh day. Therefore the Lord blessed the Sabbath day and made it holy.

5. Honor your father and your mother, so that you may live long in the land the Lord your God is giving you.

6. You shall not murder.

7. You shall not commit adultery.

8. You shall not steal.

9. You shall not give false testimony against your neighbor.

10. You shall not covet your neighbor's house. You shall not covet your neighbor's wife, or his manservant or maidservant, his ox or donkey, or anything that belongs to your neighbor." Exodus 20:1-17

When you read these Commandments, you most likely experience thoughts or emotions like the following:

-"You've got to be kidding! No one can keep these Commandments!"

-"These are ridiculous! God must have given these Commandments to this ancient people because they weren't as advanced as our civilization."

-"These Commandments may have applied to Moses, but they must not apply to us ... besides who ever heard of not working on Sunday."

-"If I had to follow these Commandments, I'd lose all my friends, and I wouldn't be any fun."

It is very difficult for the modern day Christian to relate to the Ten Commandments. Throughout the Bible, God makes it clear that He does want us to follow His Commandments. About 400 years after Moses, Solomon reinforced this as he summarized in the book of Ecclesiastes:

"Now all has been heard; here is the conclusion of the matter: Fear God and keep His Commandments, for this is the whole duty of man. For God will bring every deed into judgment, including every hidden thing, whether it is good or evil." Ecclesiastes 12:13-14

Jesus also made his position clear when he said:

"Do not think that I have come to abolish the Law or the Prophets; I have not come to abolish them but to fulfill them. I tell you the truth, until heaven and earth disappear, not the smallest letter, nor the least stroke of a pen, will by any means disappear from the Law until everything is accomplished. Anyone who breaks one of the least of these Commandments and teaches others to do the same will be called least in the kingdom of heaven, but whoever practices and teaches these Commandments will be called great in the kingdom of heaven." Matthew 5:17-19

Jesus acknowledged that some of the Commandments were greater than the others, as well as the basis for others. He went into this when he was asked the following question by a Pharisee:

"Teacher, which is the greatest Commandment in the Law?' Jesus replied: 'Love the Lord with all your soul and with all your mind. This is the first and greatest Commandment. And the second is like it: Love your neighbor as yourself. All the Law and Prophets hang on these two Commandments." Matthew 22:36-40

Following God's directives whether today, in Moses' time or in Jesus' time, is and has not been easy. The next four chapters are intended to share with you what I have discovered on this matter.

11

SIN

"If we claim to be without sin, we deceive ourselves and the truth is not in us." I John 1:8

What is sin? Sin is transgressing the Law of God. Paul is more explicit in his letter to the Galatians:

"The acts of the sinful nature are obvious: sexual immorality, impurity and debauchery; idolatry and witchcraft; hatred, discord, jealousy, fits of rage, selfish ambition, dissentions, factions and envy; drunkenness, orgies, and the like. I warn you, as I did before, that those who live like this will not inherit the kingdom of God." Galatians 5:19-21

God, our creator, has allowed us to choose our actions with our own free will. In other words, and within the confines of our governments, we can do what we please. Just because we live within man's law, however, doesn't mean that we live within God's law. Again, Paul offered some wisdom along this line:

"You, my brothers, were called to be free. But do not use your freedom to indulge the sinful nature; rather, serve one another in love. The entire law is summed up in a single command: 'Love your neighbor as yourself.'" Galatians 5:13-14

Our own free will allows us to sin. Unfortunately, sinning is attractive to us. When you choose to sin, God did not cause you to do it … you can only blame yourself.

"When tempted, no one should say 'God is tempting me.' For God cannot be tempted by evil, nor does He tempt anyone; but each one is tempted when, by his own evil desire, he is dragged away and enticed. Then after desire has conceived, it gives birth to sin; and sin, when it is full-grown, gives birth to death." James 1:13-15

"Those controlled by the sinful nature cannot please God." Romans 8:8

The Bible certainly speaks out about and against sin. The entire Old Testament deals with the ups and downs of the Jewish nation that result from obeying or not obeying God. Their fortunes were a direct result of not sinning or sinning.

Preaching about sin doesn't sell. Most people do not want to be told what bad sinners they are ... particularly when they are told by another man or woman. We all have our faults and our sins. Preaching about them may be interpreted as passing judgment on your fellow man or conveying a "holier than thou" attitude. Most people try to avoid receiving this type of criticism at all costs.

On the other hand, most people believe in God; and they do desire to be taught about Him. By learning about God and becoming closer to Him, people become more aware of their sinfulness. Awareness of sin is the first step toward correcting it. Sin is frequently attractive as well as habit forming! Change is difficult, but it is very possible to change when it is your decision to do so.

Jesus reprimanded the Pharisees about this very thing. On one occasion when Jesus was being questioned about following one of the many man-made rituals, he was very specific:

"Jesus replied, 'And you experts in the Law, woe to you, because you load people down with burdens they can hardly carry, and you yourselves will not lift one finger to help them." Luke 11:46

Later Jesus went further to point out the sins of the Pharisees when he said:

"No servant can serve two masters. Either he will hate the one and love the other, or he will be devoted to the one and despise the other. You cannot serve both God and money.' The Pharisees, who loved money, heard all this and were sneering at Jesus. He said to them, 'You are the ones who justify yourselves in the eyes of men, but God knows your hearts. What is highly valued among men is detestable in God's sight." Luke 16:13-15

Telling other people about their sins is a form of judging them. Most people when judged take the opportunity to do the same. Jesus explained this:

"Do not judge, or you too will be judged. For in the same way you judge others, you will be judged, and with the measure you use, it will be measured to you. Why do you look at the speck of sawdust in your brother's eye and pay no attention to the plank in your own eye?" Matthew 7:1-4

Sin is real and definitely exists in each of our lives. If we want to be closer to God, we must concern ourselves with sin. Fortunately, God has given us the means to handle our sins. Jesus and the New Testament provide us with a remarkably easy means of seeking forgiveness for our sins and, equally important, a way of enlisting God's help in avoiding repeat performances.

"For Christ died for our sins once for all, the righteous for the unrighteous, to bring you to God. He was put to death in the body but made alive by the Spirit." I Peter 3:18

Paul gives an excellent discourse on sin in his letter to Romans. I suggest that you read Romans 5:12 through 6:23.

12

FORGIVING, LOVING GOD

As I mentioned before, the Bible is a history of the struggles between man and God. God gave us free will, and since Adam we have persisted in misusing that freedom. Going against the will of God is sin.

In the Bible God declares repeatedly that He loves us and that He is willing to forgive us of our sins. As far back as Exodus God explained His nature to Moses:

"...The Lord, the Lord, the compassionate and gracious God, slow to anger, abounding in love and faithfulness, maintaining love to thousands, and forgiving wickedness, rebellion and sin ..." Exodus 34:6-7

Prior to the coming of Christ, God provided for men to obtain forgiveness for our sins through offerings and sacrifices. This process is called atonement, and it is discussed further in the next chapter.

The important point arising from the Old Testament was simply that God is willing to forgive us our sins. He forgives us because He loves us. "You are forgiving and good, O Lord, abounding in love to all who call to you." Psalm 86:5

"Dear friends, let us love one another, for love comes from God. Everyone who loves has been born of God and knows God." I John 4:7

Christ emphasized the importance of love to the Father: "This is my command: Love each other." John 15:17

In a world that is full of hate and violence, isn't it refreshing that the creator God – the infinite, omnipotent Being - is loving and forgiving?

God is willing to love all of us … regardless of our sins. In order for His love to really work within us, however, we must seek His forgiveness for our sins. My intent for this brief chapter is to point out that receiving God's love coincides with and is dependent upon receiving His forgiveness. Because we continue to sin, we must continue to request and obtain His forgiveness.

Why bother? Well that is entirely up to you. But the opposite of righteousness and holiness is wickedness and immorality. The former two come with the promise of peace of mind and eternal life. The latter come with turmoil, strife and eternal damnation.

13

SACRIFICES – OFFERINGS – ATONEMENT

Some sections of the Old Testament dwell heavily on sacrifices, offerings and atonement. At times, this is to the point of distracting the reader. Understanding why this process existed will help you get through these sections. More importantly, this understanding will help you know why Christ came into this world.

From the beginning of time, God has been pleased by certain offerings. In general, He demanded that offerings be made. He also insisted that they have significant value to the person giving the offering. The gift is very personal and is measured in relation to what each individual could have given.

One example of this is the relative acceptability of the offerings presented by Cain and Abel (Adam's sons). Cain's offering of some of the grain he grew was apparently only a token of his total crop. On the other hand, Abel's offering of his firstborn sheep was more significant in relation to his total flock.

"Now Abel kept flocks and Cain worked the soil. In the course of time Cain brought some of the fruits of the soil as an offering to the Lord. But Abel brought fat portions from some of the firstborn of his flock. The Lord looked with favor on Abel and his offering, but on Cain and his offering he did not look with favor, and his face was downcast.

Then the Lord said to Cain, 'Why are you angry? Why is your face downcast? If you do what is right, will you not be accepted? But if you do not do what is right, sin is crouching at your door; it desires to have you, but you must master it." Genesis 4:1-7

Jesus illustrates the personal aspect of what each man gives to God in the following:

"Jesus sat down opposite the place where the offerings were put and watched the crowd putting their money into the temple treasury. Many rich people threw in large amounts. But a poor widow came and put in two very small copper coins, worth only a fraction of a penny. Calling his disciples to him, Jesus said, 'I tell you the truth, this poor widow has put more into the treasury than all the others. They all gave out of their wealth; but she, out of her poverty, put in everything – all she had to live on." Mark 12:41-44

Simply put, through offerings man is giving back to God a portion of what God has given to us – a "thank you" for the blessings that have been bestowed upon us.

Sacrifices, on the other hand, were to atone for sinful behavior. The sacrifices made were given as a consequence of men's actions. By having free choice, man sinned against God and the sacrifice was demanded by God in order for man to get back in His good grace. To help in your understanding, compare the definitions:

Sacrifice - The act of giving up something of value for the sake of something of greater value.
Atonement - The act of making amends or reparation. Satisfaction of wrongdoing.

A great portion of the instruction or law presented in Leviticus, Numbers, and Deuteronomy deals with offering proper sacrifices and atoning for specific sins.

Over the years covered by the Old Testament, the Jews took offering sacrifices and seeking atonement to exceedingly great lengths. We find that there were "show-offs" who offered great sacrifices and cheaters offering worthless sacrifices. There were sacrifices made to gods or idols other than the Lord. Frequently, there were no sacrifices offered when there should have been. The entire process became distorted; and as a result, God's purpose was distorted as well.

In other words, the sacrificial system of the Old Testament became too difficult. Men, including priests, distorted and perverted the system and its purpose. After centuries of this behavior, God seems to have said; "Okay, that's it! I'm going to allow one last perfect sacrifice to end all this ridiculous behavior. Henceforth, all you will have to do to be forgiven for your sins is to simply ask forgiveness in My son's name."

As the Apostle Peter told the Gentiles about Jesus:

"All the prophets testify about him that everyone who believes in him receives forgiveness of sins through his name." Acts 10:43

It is consistent with God's unchanging nature that a sacrifice was made to obtain forgiveness of sins. Jesus, who was God's son and without sin, became the sacrifice for the sins of the entire world – Jews and gentiles. As the Apostle John wrote:

"My dear children, I write this to you so that you will not sin. But if anybody does sin, we have one who speaks to the Father in our defense – Jesus Christ, the Righteous One. He is the atoning sacrifice for our sins, and not only for ours but also for the sins of the whole world." I John 2:1-2

And that's how it now stands. We all still sin; and every time that we do, to obtain God's forgiveness we just have to ask for it ... no sacrifices, just prayer (see Chapters 18 and 24 for some qualifications).

"If we claim to be without sin, we deceive ourselves and the truth in not in us. If we confess our sins, He is faithful and just and will forgive us our sins and purify us from all unrighteousness." I John 1:8-9

And summing it all up from another passage in John's first letter:

"This is how God showed his love among us: He sent His one and only son into the world that we might live through him. This is love: not that we loved God, but that He loved us and sent His son as an atoning sacrifice for our sins." I John 4:9-12

14

Jesus Christ

Our family has moved several times. On one of these moves and following the inevitable "shopping" for a church, we were going through the orientation program for new members. The minister asked each of us to write down what Jesus Christ meant to us individually. I don't remember exactly what I wrote, but it was something to do with Jesus being a good example and that he told us how God wanted us to act. Although the minister did not tell me, my answer was way off the mark, and subconsciously I knew it. The question haunted me for several years thereafter.

Indeed, Jesus was the greatest man that ever lived. But, he was also a great deal more.

The following was what Jesus said about himself:

"I am the way and the truth and the life. No one comes to the Father except through me." John 14:6

Paul gave a short biography of Christ in his letter to the Philippians:

"Who being in very nature God, did not consider equality with God something to be grasped, but made himself nothing, taking the very nature of a servant, being made in human likeness. And being found in appearance as a man, he humbled himself and became obedient to death – even death on a cross! Therefore God exalted him to the highest place and gave him the name that is above every name, that at the name of Jesus every knee should bow, in heaven and earth and under the earth, and every tongue confess that Jesus Christ is Lord, to the Glory of God the Father." Philippians 2:6-11

Jesus Christ is the Son of God; he is our personal savior; he is the fulfillment of Old Testament prophesies; he enables everyone to receive salvation and eternal life; and finally, he will be the judge of all mankind upon his second coming. This is quite a list of credentials! Let's look at these one at a time:

Son of God
Jesus was born of a virgin. His father was God. This was prophesized by Isaiah 700 years before the birth of Christ:

"Therefore the Lord Himself will give you a sign; The virgin will be with child and will give birth to a son, and will call him Immanuel." Isaiah 7:14

In the gospel of John, Jesus is quoted and testifies to being the son of God:

"For God so loved the world that He gave His one and only son, that whoever believes in him shall have eternal life." John 3:16

Peter witnesses to Christ's authority and being God's son:

"We did not follow cleverly invented stories when we told you about the power and coming of our Lord Jesus Christ, but were eyewitnesses of his majesty. For he received honor and glory from God the Father when the voice came to him from the Majestic Glory, saying, 'This is my son, whom I love; with him I am well pleased.' We ourselves heard this voice that came from heaven when we were with him on the sacred mountain." 2 Peter 1:16-18

Personal Savior
Through Christ every individual can obtain God's blessing and be forgiven of their sins. Jesus spoke of his mission:

"For God did not send His son into the world to condemn the world, but to save the world through him. Whoever believes in him is not condemned, but whoever does not believe stands condemned already because he has not believed in the name of God's one and only son." John 3:17-18

Paul wrote about how Christ is our intermediary to God in his letter to Romans: "But now righteousness from God, apart from the law, has been made known, to which the Law and the Prophets testify. This righteousness from God comes through faith in Jesus Christ to all who believe. There is no difference, for all have sinned and fall short of the glory of God, and are justified freely by His grace through the redemption that came by Christ Jesus." Romans 3:21-24

In the letter to Hebrews, it is spelled out how faith in Christ will bring salvation:

"Just as man is destined to die once, and after that to face judgment, so Christ was sacrificed once to take away the sins of many people; and he will appear a second time, not to bear sin, but to bring salvation to those who are waiting for him." Hebrews 9:27-28

Fulfillment of Old Testament

There were many prophesies in the Old Testament that were fulfilled by Christ. His life, his death and his resurrection were all foretold. The New Testament writers, particularly Matthew, cite specific passages of the Old Testament scripture that were fulfilled in Jesus. This fulfillment was the authority that brought thousands of early Jews to Christianity. The Jews were knowledgeable of the Old Testament scripture and realized that Jesus was the expected Messiah by virtue of him fulfilling the scriptures.

"Do not think that I come to abolish the Law or the Prophets; I have not come to abolish them but to fulfill them." Matthew 5:17

There are many references to the Messiah throughout the Old Testament. The following is a short list of passages you can crosscheck between the Old and New Testaments:

Old Testament	New Testament
Isaiah 7:14	Matthew 1:22
Micah 5:2	Luke 2:4
Malachi 3:1	Luke 7:24
Isaiah 40:3	Luke 3:4
Deuteronomy 18:15	Acts 3:20
Zechariah 9:9	Mark 11:7
Zechariah 11:12	Matthew 26:15
Isaiah 53:7	Mark 15:4
Psalm 69:21	Matthew 27:34
Psalm 22:17	Matthew 27:35
Psalm 34:20	John 19:32

There are many other passages pointed out in most study guides which you can examine if you are so inclined. The point being made, however, is that from Genesis to Malachi and over a period of several hundred years God foretold to the Jews certain things that were to be fulfilled in Christ. Again, the fulfillment of scripture by Jesus validated to the devout, early Jews that he was who he said he was.

One of the best summaries of the miraculous nature of Jesus' coming to us is by a deceased British pastor, author and editor of a Christian magazine named David M. Panton:

The most amazing drama that ever was presented to the mind of man – a drama written in prophecy in the Old Testament and in biography in the four Gospels of the New Testament – is the narrative of Jesus the Christ. One outstanding fact, among many, completely isolates Him. It is this: that one man only in the history of the world has had explicit details given beforehand of His birth, life, death and resurrection; that these details are in documents given to the public centuries before He appeared, and that no one challenges, or can challenge, that these documents were widely circulated long before His birth; and that anyone and everyone can compare for himself the actual records of His life with those ancient documents, and find that they match one another perfectly.[1]

Extended Salvation to All

Jesus was the fulfillment of scripture. However, the one big event that got the attention of the Jews as well as brought Gentiles to Christianity was Christ's resurrection from the dead. This confirmed God's promise of everlasting life.

As we touched on in Chapter 5, up until the coming of Christ the Jews were the chosen people of God. With few exceptions, only those Jews who pleased God were entitled to everlasting life. Through Jesus and the New Testament, God has expanded His invitation to all people.

Jesus spoke of this:

"I tell you the truth, whoever hears my words and believes Him who sent me has eternal life and will not be condemned; he has crossed over from death to life." John 5:24

Peter, with the help of the Holy Spirit, clarified the inclusion of non-Jews by God in His invitation when Peter was speaking to the apostles about the Gentiles:

"So if God gave them the same gift as He gave us, who believed in the Lord Jesus Christ, who was I to think that I could oppose God?' When they heard this, they had no further objections and praised God, saying, 'So then, God has granted even Gentiles repentance unto life." Acts 11:17-18 The gift that Peter speaks about is the gift of the Holy Spirit.

Whether you are a Jew or you are not, whether you know and follow the Law of Moses or you do not, these are not the critical determining factors when it comes to

[1] D. M. Panton, *The Judgement Seat of Christ*, (London, C. J. Thynne and Jarvis Ltd., ca. 1927).

obtaining eternal salvation. In other words, through Jesus Christ, God has removed the burden of doubt associated with "pass or fail" when being judged by the Law as set forth in the Old Testament.

Judge upon the Second Coming

Jesus' promised second coming is the one area of prophesy in both the Old and the New Testaments that has yet to be fulfilled. It is clear from the Bible that he will come again ... exactly when and how are not clear. The next chapter deals more with this subject.

In closing, believing in Jesus Christ and doing his will is what God wants us to do. Peter talked about this when he told others what the resurrected Jesus told him: "He commanded us to preach to the people and to testify that he is the one whom God appointed as judge of the living and the dead. All the prophets testify about him that everyone who believes in him receives forgiveness of sins through his name." Acts 10:42-43

15

The Second Coming of Christ

Moses, the Psalmists and the Prophets all foretold the coming of Christ the Messiah. They also foretold of the Lord's final judgment. Because this latter event has not happened, it is difficult to tell exactly from the Bible when and precisely how it will occur. But, since everything else foretold in the Bible has come true, we can be certain that there will be a final judgment.

Conceivably, if we knew exactly when the final judgment were coming, we could live with our sins up until the last minute, repent and ask forgiveness just in time to save our souls. God gave us free will to choose our own life (and fate), but He did not give us a sense for His timing. The time frame for God's final judgment may not be meaningful relative to the short time-frame of our own individual lives. In other words, many people think that they will probably die before having to face God's final judgment ... but we don't know that for certain.

Once we reach adulthood, medically speaking we die a little each day. We know we are dying, but we just don't know when. You have probably heard about people who turn to God and ask for forgiveness when they know they are about to die.

The thought of our death makes us each think about how we will fare with God's final judgment ..."it's up to you." Whether we live to a ripe old age or whether God's judgment occurs in our lifetime, these are not really the point. The Bible tells us that we will *all* be judged, and we will be judged within *God's* timeframe. Therefore this judgment will occur before or after we die.

It is also clear from the Bible that God's final judgment and Christ's second coming are linked together. Bible theologians disagree on the order of events, but they do agree that Christ will return and that he will be the judge!

Jesus talked about his second coming in the gospels:

"For the Son of Man is going to come in his Father's glory with His angels, and then he will reward each person according to what he has done." Matthew 16:27

"No one knows about that day or hour, not even the angels in heaven, nor the Son, but only the Father. As it was in the days of Noah, so it will be at the coming of the Son of Man." Matthew 24:36-37

"When the Son of Man comes in glory, and all the angels with him, he will sit on his throne in heavenly glory." Matthew 25:31

"If anyone is ashamed of me and my words in this adulterous and sinful generation, the Son of Man will be ashamed of him when he comes in his Father's glory with the holy angels." Mark 8:38

"At that time they will see the Son of Man coming in a cloud with power and great glory." Luke 21:27

Upon his second coming, Christ will be the judge. Paul gives testimony to this:

"For He has set a day when He will judge the world with justice by the man He has appointed. He has given proof of this to all men by raising him from the dead." Acts 17:30-31

And Jesus testified about being that judge:

"I tell you the truth, a time is coming and has now come when the dead will hear the voice of the Son of God and those who hear will live. … And He has given him authority to judge because he is the Son of Man." John 5:25, 27

John also recounted in REVELATION what Christ said to him when he appeared to John several years after Christ's crucifixion:

"When I saw him, I fell at his feet as though dead. Then he placed his right hand on me and said: 'Do not be afraid. I am the First and the Last. I am the Living One; I was dead, and behold I am alive for ever and ever! And I hold the keys of death and Hades." Revelation 1:17-18

"Behold, I am coming soon! My reward is with me, and I will give to everyone according to what he has done. I am the Alpha and the Omega, the First and the Last, the Beginning and the End." Revelation 22:12-13

The last prophesy of Malachi in the last book of the Old Testament talked about the final judgment: "Surely the day is coming; it will burn like a furnace. All the arrogant and every evildoer will be stubble, and that day that is coming will set them on fire,' says the Lord Almighty." Malachi 4:1

16

GOD IS NOT A PUSHOVER

There are common misconceptions that God is a gentle being and that Christians prefer love over force in all circumstances. In my opinion, this arises from two factors:

-"The Golden Rule" states that you should love your neighbor as yourself; and

-God sent His son into the world as an extremely humble man of a very impoverished family. Jesus' earthly ministry used no force. (On the contrary, Jewish historians anticipated a great leader coming in grand style with plenty of "muscle" to back him up.)

God through Moses and Jesus told us to love our fellow men. However, the first and most important commandment is to love God.

Christ was humble and poor, but he also could be firm and threatening when he witnessed sinful behavior. Perhaps one of Christ's most well-known actions was to drive out the money-changers from the Temple (Mark 11:15). He drove out those merchants who were profiting from and commercializing God's sacrificial system.

Less well known, Jesus was also very firm in his dealing with the religious leaders when he accused them of hypocritical behavior:

"The teachers of the Law and Pharisees sit in Moses' seat. So you must obey them and do everything they tell you. But do not do what they do, for they do not practice what they preach. They tie up heavy loads and put them on men's shoulders, but they themselves are not willing to lift a finger to move them. ... You snakes! You brood of vipers! How will you escape being condemned to hell?" Matthew 23:2-4, 33

God does deal with sin. He makes it clear to us that we will each be accountable to Him for all of our sins. Most of us expect this judgment after we die. Throughout the Bible God has dealt with sin before death too.

Way back in the time of Moses, Aaron (Moses' brother) was the chief priest. Aaron's sons "inherited" the right to follow their father into the priesthood. Two of his sons, Nadab and Abihu, were not taking their priestly responsibilities seriously; and the Lord killed them on the spot. (Leviticus 10)

In the early Christian church, Ananias and Sapphira pledged to God to give some property to Him. They knowingly held back after committing it all. God struck them dead when Peter confronted them. Acts 5

Before Moses and in the time of Abraham, the cities of Sodom and Gomorrah were so sinful and without any righteous people that God destroyed the complete cities. Genesis 18:16-19, 29

The point of these examples is that God's judgment can occur whenever *He* pleases.

Our concern should be that a negative judgment from God does not end in our death, but continues on into eternity. The Bible is fairly explicit that if we do not go on to eternal life, the alternative is *not* that we simply cease to exist. The alternative is punishment into eternity. If you think about this prospect, it's grim!

Jesus makes it clear that hell exists and that it is both miserable and enduring:

"...It is better for you to enter life with one eye that to have two eyes and be thrown into the fire of hell." Matthew 18:9

"...Depart from me, you who are cursed, into the eternal fire prepared for the devil and his angels." "...Then they will go away to eternal punishment, but the righteous to eternal life." Matthew 25:41, 46

In Jude's letter, he expounds on the doom of godless men:

"In a similar way, Sodom and Gomorrah and the surrounding towns gave themselves up to sexual immorality and perversion. They serve as an example of those who suffer the punishment of eternal fire." Jude 7

Jesus also advises us to be careful. When he sent out his disciples, he cautioned them:

"I am sending you out like sheep among wolves. Therefore be as shrewd as snakes and as innocent as doves." Matthew 10:16

Jesus told his disciples to be prepared for the worst when he told them that the gospel of love and peace that they were to preach would bring violence:

"Do not suppose that I have come to bring peace to the earth. I did not come to bring peace, but a sword." Matthew 10:34

Do not underestimate the Lord's willingness to deal with a problem *right* away … in the here and now! God is no pushover when it comes to sin.

17

THE CONCEPT OF THE TRINITY

Basically, the Trinity is not spelled out in the Bible. The word Trinity is not mentioned specifically in the Bible either. The term Trinity represents three persons in one ... the Father, the Son and the Holy Spirit. The Bible does talk about each of these "persons" in the context of being God. Interestingly enough, the Bible does not limit God to these three persons.

In the first centuries after the crucifixion of Christ, the early Christian church grappled with the issue of one God with different persons or forms. They stated their beliefs in the form of creeds. Two such creeds that you may be familiar with are the Nicene and the Apostles' Creeds. If you wish to study the early church's definition of the Trinity (which still holds), I'd suggest reading through these creeds. You can Google either of these creeds online, but the related excerpts are as follows:

"I believe in God the Father Almighty ... And in Jesus Christ his only Son our Lord ... I believe in the Holy Ghost ..."

In layman's terms, the Trinity is as follows:

Father: This is God, our Lord. This is the infinite, omnipotent, omnipresent being that created the universe and all things in it.

Son: This is Jesus Christ (Chapter 14). He is the perfect example of what the Father wanted man to be. He is also the only man without sin and was sacrificed for all our sins.

After his crucifixion, the Son took on all the power of God and will come again to inherit and judge the earth.

Holy Spirit (Ghost): This being dwells ever-present in those that accept Jesus Christ as their savior. Prior to Jesus, God apparently only gave the Holy Spirit to select individuals. Now we may all enjoy the Spirit. The Holy Spirit is our guiding light to understanding God's word; he is our conscience directing us to do what God wants of us; and as well, he keeps us attuned to differentiating right from wrong.

Jesus told his disciples about the Holy Spirit as well as the interrelationship of the persons that make up the Trinity in the Gospel of John:

"If you love me, you will obey what I command. And I will ask the Father, and He will give you another Counselor to be with you forever – the Spirit of Truth. The world cannot accept him, for he lives with you and will be in you. I will not leave you as orphans; I will come to you. Before long, the world will not see me anymore, but you will see me. Because I live, you also will live. On that day you will realize that I am in my Father, and you are in me, and I am in you. Whoever has my commands and obeys them, he is the one who loves me. He who loves me will be loved by my Father, and I too will love him and show myself to him." John 14: 15-21

The concept of the Trinity is very basic Christian theology. It is also very important theology. Because the Trinity is not spelled out more clearly in the Bible, this particular doctrine is and has been subject to faulty interpretation (see Chapter 20).

I must also add that the Trinity may be difficult doctrine to understand. If it is for you, I suggest you consider comparing God to water. Water exists in three very different forms – ice, liquid and steam. All three forms are water. Obviously, God is not water, but the illustration may help to expand your thought process when thinking about the Trinity.

18

BORN AGAIN

Perhaps you have overheard the following conversation:

Jim Osostraight: "Are you a Christian?"

Matt Hardworker, in reply: "Well yes ... I go to church; my mother raised me to believe."

Osostraight, sounding a wee bit haughty: "I mean, are you a *born again* Christian?"

Matt, slightly overcome by buzz words and somewhat intimidated: "Well, I guess I don't know exactly what you mean ..."

What precisely do these charged up, sometimes overzealous people mean by Born Again?

The phrase Born Again is a quote from Jesus found in Chapter 3 of John. Jesus said: "I tell you the truth, no one can see the kingdom of God unless he is born again." John 3:3

Jesus was talking about receiving the Holy Spirit through voluntarily accepting and believing in Jesus Christ as your Lord and personal savior. He meant making God the number one priority in your life. This involves committing to love the Lord your God with all your heart and with all your soul and with all your mind.

Receiving Christ and becoming Born Again is very much between you and Him. Fortunately, it is freely offered to all people. It doesn't involve the ritual of joining a fraternity or the publicized testimony of accepting public office. It is very personal and simple matter of trusting in the Lord and turning your life over to Him.

By accepting Christ and belonging to God, your ability to understand His will increases:

"He who belongs to God hears what God says. The reason you do not hear is that you do not belong to God." John 8:47

By belonging to God, your body becomes a "temple" for the Holy Spirit. With God dwelling in your body, you become responsible for how you treat His temple. Paul wrote about this responsibility:

"Don't you know that you yourselves are God's temple and that God's Spirit lives in you? If anyone destroys God's temple, God will destroy him; for God's temple is sacred, and you are that temple." I Corinthians 3:16-17

Being Born Again is achieved by committing yourself to God. Unless it is God's specific will for you, being Born Again is not standing on a street corner making a fool of yourself. Jesus cautioned against public displays of prayer:

"And when you pray, do not be like the hypocrite, for they love to pray standing in the synagogues and on the street corners to be seen by men. I tell you the truth, they have received their reward in full. But when you pray, go into your room, close the door and pray to your Father, who is unseen." Matthew 6:5-6

To most people, being born again was or is a non-event as far as the outside world (other people) is concerned. It is a personal reorganizing of priorities to get your priorities in line with God's will for you. Trust in God, He will not make you into a fool!

19

Is There Really a Devil?

You better believe that there is a Devil! Not only is there a Devil, it appears from scripture that the Devil *also* has demons that help him in his work. Sound scary? Without Christ to help you, it certainly can be.

The Bible identifies the Devil by many titles, such as Satan, the Evil One, the Serpent in the Garden of Eden, the Fallen Angel, the Prince of Darkness, etc. It appears that the Devil has superhuman (and supernatural) powers; but his powers are limited by God. The Evil One has powers less than God but definitely greater than the powers of men. As such, the Devil is clearly a force to be reckoned with on this earth. As John puts it:

"We know that we are children of God, and that the whole world is under the control of the Evil One." I John 5:19

Although the Devil is called the ruler of this earth, he is not a ruler of heaven. Fortunately God has restrained him from certain acts – mainly from inflicting spiritual harm to those who have accepted Christ.

Christians need to be aware of Satan; but they have nothing to fear from him. Put another way, the Holy Spirit and Satan cannot dwell in the same body.

As real as the Devil is, sin is ours; that is, we are all sinners. The Devil is *not* always pushing us to sin … we help ourselves in this regard. Because we all sin of our own free will, we need to be careful to avoid blaming that there is a devil responsible for our sinful acts. "The Devil made me do it" can be a cop out.

Equal to giving the Devil more credit that he is due, we must avoid falling into the trap of classifying, or judging, those people that are different from us as being evil. This is not a completely right and wrong world. Obviously if it were, *everyone* would want to be on the side of right. So when you're feeling particularly righteous, be careful not to judge others as evil.

Back to the point of this chapter ... the Devil is the direct cause of some of the evil in this world. Furthermore, the Devil is out to disrupt Christianity (as well as humanity).

There should be great comfort that, as a Christian, the supernatural cannot harm you. That is not to say that another person under the influence of Satan or Satanic forces could not inflict physical harm to you. It is simply to say that frightening, unknown things that moviemakers seem to delight in – aliens, voodoo, ghosts, magic, etc. – cannot invade and overcome the soul of a Christian.

Recapitulating from scripture, we are told that Satan leads the world away from God:

"... they lost their place in heaven. The great dragon was hurled down – that ancient serpent called the devil or Satan, who leads the whole world astray ..." Revelation 12:8-9

Especially recent or new converts to Christianity are subject to distraction by Satan. This is brought out by Paul when he pointed out that for church office, a "seasoned" Christian is necessary:

"He must not be a recent convert, or he may become conceited and fall under the same judgment as the devil." I Timothy 3:6

By holding firm to God and resisting Satan, Satan will go away:

"Submit yourselves, then, to God. Resist the devil, and he will flee from you. Come near to God and He will come near to you." James 4:7-8

Be continually reminded that Satan is always nearby to tempt you:

"Be self-controlled and alert. Your enemy the devil prowls around like a roaring lion looking for someone to devour." I Peter 5:8

Jesus spoke of the Devil's role in this world as well as the Devil's character. First, in the parable of the sower:

"A farmer went out to sow his seed. As he was scattering the seed, some fell along the path; it was trampled on, and the birds of the air ate it up." Luke 8:5 "This is the meaning of the parable: The seed is the word of God. Those along the path are the ones who hear, and then the devil comes and takes away the word from their hearts, so that they may not believe and be saved." Luke 8:11-12

Jesus chastises the Pharisees at one point indicating He is aware that the Devil has influenced them:

"Why is my language not clear to you? Because you are unable to hear what I say. You belong to your father, the devil, and you want to carry out your father's desire. He was a murderer from the beginning, not holding to the truth, for there is no truth in him. When he lies, he speaks his native language, for he is a liar and the father of lies." John 8:43-44

Jesus talked of His return and the final judgment:

"When the Son of Man comes in His glory, and all the angels with him, he will sit on His throne in heavenly glory. All the nations will be gathered before Him, and He will separate the people one from another as a shepherd separates the sheep from the goats. He will put the sheep on His right and the goats on His left." Matthew 25:31-33 "Then He will say to those on His left, 'Depart from me, you who are cursed, into the eternal fire prepared for the devil and his angels." Matthew 25:41

Certainly we should all aspire to be His sheep and placed on His right!

20

WATCH OUT FOR BAD DOCTRINE!

The world abounds with false teachers and bad doctrine. This exists today as it always has. Bad doctrine usually is a manifestation of a cult. A cult, in turn, is a religious movement usually founded by a powerful and gifted individual who distorts the Biblical message by adding something more to it. A cult may proclaim belief in Jesus Christ and the Bible, but invariably, they will take their cult's beliefs beyond God's word with their own interpretations or additional authorities. These interpretations or additional authorities are contrary to Christian tradition. The best way for you and me to be able to identify a cult is for us to study and gain our own understanding of the Bible and its message.

A cult usually does not outwardly claim to be a cult. They generally will not lead off with a statement of their differences with Christianity. The cult members you may encounter probably don't completely understand their religion themselves!

I am not an expert on cults. However, like most people, I can feel when I'm being baited or pushed too hard to purchase or agree to something. Some religious groups can be very overbearing. Basically, when confronted with what might seem to be bad doctrine or cultic practice, you should test their precepts with the unadulterated, time-tested Bible. The Bible is understandable as well as being the final authority in these matters.

The Christian Research Institute of Charlotte, North Carolina is a self-proclaimed and generally accepted authority on cults. You might contact them with difficult questions or for information on groups or doctrine that may be confusing you. They are very helpful. Their website is www.equip.org.

Certainly not all cults contain "weird people." In fact, some cults are made up of very good people. When you are not a Biblical expert, it is very difficult to know what is consistent with God and what is not.

The entire second chapter of 2 Peter is devoted to making us aware of the existence of false teachers. You may want to read it.

A cult may claim a very positive interpretation of God. Thus they become the only true authority. Some cults play upon our inquisitive instincts by being secretive, bizarre or extraordinarily composed and self-confident.

Generally, there are two types of cults. One variety starts with Biblical doctrine and adeptly moves away from God's word toward the certain cult's own theory. The challenge in these instances is to pinpoint exactly how they stray from God's word.

The second variety of cult is best described as being secretive. If their beliefs and doctrines are not fully disclosed at your asking, be *very* careful. In fact, you should be more that careful; you should probably get away as soon as possible!

You should seek outside counsel before making a commitment or joining a religious group. It doesn't hurt to take the time to check them out … you certainly would be cautious if you were making a large purchase (car, home, etc.). You should be equally cautious when involving your relationship with God and eternity!

Again, the best defense to bad doctrine is to tests it with God's word – the Bible.

21

MIRACLES

Throughout the Old and New Testaments, God used several means to substantiate the validity of His word as well as His existence. The most well-known means were miracles. However, He also gave supernatural powers to some people; and He certainly spoke directly through the prophets. These may not have been miracles, per se; but they were certainly miraculous.

Well known miracles were the parting of the Red Sea for Moses (Exodus 14); the giving of daily manna to the Jews in the wilderness for forty years so that they did not starve (Exodus 16); the bringing back to life from death of Lazarus (John 11); and the feeding of the five thousand by Jesus with a few fish and little bread (Matthew 14).

Well known powers given by God were King Solomon's wisdom (1 Kings 3), Sampson's strength (Judges 13), and the undefeatable armies of Moses, Joshua and King David.

Prophets played a very important role in the history of the Old Testament. The prophets were called upon to petition God on various matters. God then spoke to or through the prophets so they could recount His words to the people. As you may recall from Chapter 8, a prophet was able to foretell future events within the prophet's own lifetime so that people would believe that the same prophet was able to predict events further into the future ... beyond the prophet's lifetime.

Whether God provided a miracle, or gave supernatural powers, or spoke through a prophet, His purpose was consistent. It not only got everyone's attention but it authenticated His word or purpose.

This authentication from God was important. One could say this process is what created the Bible. Within the many books of the Bible, this authentication from God existed either through the author of the book (so the author was known to be God's man – so to speak) or existed through events recounted in each book (the miracles, the supernatural powers or the prophet's words). For us today, the test of time has proven the Bible. But during the thousand plus years that scripture was being put together, miracles played a very important role.

22

GREAT STORIES IN THE BIBLE

There are some absolutely great stories in the Bible. They read well, are entertaining, and pass most literary tests. Some of the better and well known stories have been dramatized by Hollywood. For this reason, most people are familiar with the main characters of these stories without having read the Bible.

I have selected slightly more than a dozen stories which I feel are particularly good. By reading them, you will not only be entertained, but they will give you a good idea of the people and history covered in the Bible.

Noah: The story of Noah and the flood are covered in Genesis 6:5 through 9:17.

Jacob: Jacob is also referred to as Israel. Today's country of Israel got its name from this patriarch. Jacob's twelve sons became the twelve tribes that comprised the ancient Hebrew nation. The story of Jacob's family centers on his son Joseph and is action packed. See Genesis 37:2 through 50:26.

Moses: The story of Moses is a real thriller. It is covered in Exodus 2:1 through 6:12; 6:28 through 12:42; and 13:17 through 14:31. Moses led the Jews out of captivity in Egypt and survived the desert wilderness to lead them to the "promised land." The parting of the Red Sea, the receiving of the Ten Commandments, the gift of manna are all parts of Moses' story.

Joshua: Read about Joshua's conquest of Jericho as the Hebrews move into the modern day Israel. Joshua Fit the

Battle of Jericho is a well-known African American spiritual song. See Joshua 1:1-11; and 5:13 through 6:27.

Sampson: Through God, Sampson had incredible strength. Read about Sampson, the Philistines and Delilah in Judges 13:1 through 16:31.

Saul: Saul became Israel's first king. Read about how God did not want Israel to have a king, i.e. absolute ruler. Reluctantly He gave in to the desires of the people of Israel in 1 Samuel 8:1 through 15:35.

David: David succeeded Saul as king, and he was definitely God's appointed man. Israel enjoyed tremendous success under this very human personality blessed by God in 1 Samuel 16:1 through 17:58. The balance of 1 Samuel and all of 2 Samuel deal with David's reign.

David and Bathsheba: One of the Bible's greatest sex scandals. See 2 Samuel 11:1 through 12:25.

Solomon: David's son and heir, Solomon lived in grand style during a relatively peaceful time in Israel's history. Solomon was purportedly the wisest man ever to live. See 1 Kings 1:28-31; 3:1-28; 4:29-34; 9:1-9; 10:1-13; and 11:41-43.

Elijah: Elijah was a very holy man of God ... a prophet. His life was very interesting and is covered in 1 Kings 16:29-34; Joshua 6:26-27; 1 Kings 16:34 through 19:21 and 2 Kings 1:1 through 2:11.

Daniel: Daniel, another holy man, was spared by God from being torn apart by lions in Daniel 1:1 through 6:28.

John the Baptist: This John's birth was foretold, and he was a real radical! (John the Baptist is different from John the Apostle.) See Luke 1:5-25; 1:57-66; 3:1-20; 7:18-23 and Matthew 6:17-29.

Jesus' Birth: Read the Christmas story and about Christ's infancy in Matthew 1:18 through 2:23 and Luke 2:21-52.

Jesus' Temptation: When Jesus was around 30 years old, he was baptized and began his ministry. He was immediately tempted by Satan. See Matthew 3:13 through 4:17.

23

REVELATION

This is the last book of the Bible and could be named "the Revelation of Jesus Christ as given to John the Apostle." Fully understanding the book's meaning remains very controversial among Christian scholars. As such, it is practically impossible for the Bible novice to read and understand the book.

The first part of Revelation includes letters or messages to the early Christian churches. Jesus, speaking to John, has some very specific words to be delivered to each of several churches. The messages are both corrective and complementary about the practices and preaching that had evolved in those churches. I might add that the messages given to these churches are timeless and could apply to churches today.

The difficult part of the Book of Revelation was written in the symbolic, prophetic language used by the prophets ... particularly Isaiah, Ezekiel and Daniel. Parts of those books, or scriptures, that deal with prophesy regarding the Messiah were explained by Jesus to his followers. To a great extent, those explanations were documented in the New Testament. When it comes to interpreting these earlier, prophetic scriptures, Biblical scholars basically agree with Jesus' explanations. On the other hand, Jesus did not explain His prophesies in Revelation (written roughly 70 years after Christ's crucifixion). The interpretation of the highly symbolic language is left up to men ... and men disagree. Men particularly disagree when there is not a higher authority to resolve matters!

Understanding Revelation requires an understanding of the entire Bible. The writing style used, the symbolism chosen, and the messages given were all consistent with earlier books in the Bible. If you are not familiar with these styles, symbols and messages, Revelation may appear as complete gibberish. In fact, that was probably how Revelation appeared to the Romans who were persecuting Christianity at the time the book was written. The Biblical novice is somewhat like the Roman authorities in this regard.

The biggest disagreement among modern day Christians regarding Revelation concerns whether the book foretold historical events that have already occurred by now, whether the book foretells events that are yet to come, whether the book restated the Biblical message of man's sinful nature and his temptation by evil, or whether Revelation was a combination of all the above. It is clear, however, that the last few words (about 22:7 to the end) deal with the second coming of Christ.

Certain facts about Revelation do seem to have the majority of opinion. They are as follows:

-The book is an account of what Jesus told John, i.e., the book was written in God's words, not John's.

-Christ will come again to judge everyone alive or deceased. At this time He will also establish God's kingdom, or reign, upon the earth.

-Knowledge of the rest of the scriptures is mandatory for the reader of Revelation to attempt an understanding of its meaning.

-The book was written by John the Apostle in the late first century. John was one of Christ's closest friends, and he was very active in the early church.

After you have struggled through Revelation the first time, I suggest that you read what others think about the various parts of the book. Instead of taking sides right away, I also suggest that you reread the book taking in to account those different viewpoints. With God's help, you will come upon what Revelation means to you.

24

WHAT'S A NEW CHRISTIAN TO DO?

If you want to become good at anything, it requires practice. I haven't found many shortcuts through life ... although I have tried. If you want to be good at your profession, you must work at it. If you want to be accomplished at a particular sport, you must work at it. If you want to be God's person, you must work at it also.

God provides us with His Spirit to help us. We must cooperate with the Holy Spirit by making opportunities for Him. We must pray, study the Bible, gather with other Christians, and do whatever else He calls us to do. The objective is the fulfillment or living up to the first and greatest commandment – you must "Love the Lord your God with all your heart and with all your soul and with all your mind." Matthew 22:37

The goal of becoming a good Christian and satisfying His will is an ongoing one. By this I mean that within His grace there are always greater goals to be achieved. We *need* goals to keep going.

How many instances can you think of that involve people deflating, or even decomposing, as a result of achieving a particular goal? Examples of these instances might include graduation, winning an event or title, retirement ... on and on. Usually the elation of achieving the goal lasts for a while, and then depression sets in as we realize that there is nothing more to achieve.

Motivational experts are continually reminding us that we need to set goals, positively go for them, and constantly reset our goals. Of course, not all goal-seeking can be healthy. We need goals, but we must be careful how we chose and pursue them.

When we are after a particularly difficult goal, one that requires a lot of time, sacrifice, and effort to achieve, we risk worshipping that goal. The risk I am talking about is that you actually become what you worship. Timeless examples of goals other than God are Money and Power.

What do you worship? What do you rely on most? What are your goals?

Your "worshipped thing," whatever you rely on most, what you spend most your time doing or thinking about *may* be your god. Taking this "other god" one step further, one of my past ministers asks these questions of you and this other god:

-Does your god love you?

-Will your god come at the end of time and give you eternal life?

God helps us with the little goals in life. He also helps us with the biggest goal – following His will. His will differs for each of us. By determining and following His will, we feel, and our lives become, very meaningful.

Strangely enough, strong optimism or success tends to separate people from God. When people have it made (so to speak), they tend to become self-sufficient and might not feel the need for Him. On the other hand, setbacks in life tend to draw people to God. When people are in their greatest need, they frequently turn to God. When all else fails, He is there to help us.

Why not keep God in there all the time? In the "wins" as well as in the "losses"? *That's* what the new Christian is to do.

When you make it really big in some aspect of your life, don't desert Him. And for certain, when the pressure builds, always know that you can trust in God … He will not desert you.

One last point I want to make regarding the consistency and the eternal nature of God. People will always let you down, but God will not. Even the best of people die, move or somehow change on you. God will not.

We are all familiar with the common adage that goes something like this …"the only thing that does not change is change itself." This is definitely true of our world and the people in it. *However*, it is not true of God. Why not hang your hat on the one thing that is unchanging and eternal?

ABOUT THE AUTHOR

John Harlow is a retired business executive living in Lake Oswego, Oregon. He retired from a 36 year career as a "money lender." The last 20 years he was the president of a banking company specializing in commercial real estate financing. He is a graduate of the University of Illinois with an undergraduate degree in Chemical Engineering, and worked for Shell Chemical Company in New Jersey and Texas. It is this engineer's curiosity and persistence that lead to his analysis and understanding of the Bible. John and his wife are founding sponsors of a daily Bible teaching radio program by Pastor Jim Andrews of Lake Bible Church in Lake Oswego, Oregon, called The Final Word. It can be accessed through its website, www.thefinalwordradio.com.